1100 1200 1300 1400 1500 1600 1700 1800 1900 2000

CANADA THROUGH TIME
Building a Nation

Kathleen Corrigan

capstone

Read Me is published by Heinemann Raintree,
an imprint of Capstone Press,
1710 Roe Crest Drive, North Mankato, Minnesota 56003

© 2016 Heinemann-Raintree
an imprint of Capstone Global Library, LLC
Chicago, Illinois

To contact Capstone please visit www.mycapstone.com

Edited by James Benefield
Designed by Philippa Jenkins
Original illustrations © Capstone Global Library Ltd 2016
Picture research by Kelly Garvin
Production by Victoria Fitzgerald
Originated by Capstone Global Library Limited
Printed and bound in China

ISBN 978 1 410 98120 2 (hardback)
19 18 17 16 15
10 9 8 7 6 5 4 3 2 1

ISBN 978 1 410 98125 7 (paperback)
19 18 17 16 15
10 9 8 7 6 5 4 3 2 1

ISBN 978 1 410 98130 1 (ebook)

Acknowledgments
Photo credits: Alamy/Niday Picture Library, 9; Capstone Press/Karon Dubke, 28, 29; Getty Images: Buenlarge/Matthew Brady, cover (top), Hulton Archive, 24, Jack Birns/The LIFE Images Collection, 21, Notman & Son/Alinari Archives, 25, Three Lions/Stringer, 16; Granger, NYC, 6; Library and Archives Canada: acc no. 1997-229-1, 8, C-081758, 26, C-00686b, 23, National Museum of Canada, PA-013416, cover (bottom), PA-012854, 27; Library of Congress/Prints and Photographs Division, 17; Newscom: akg-images, 10; North Wind Picture Archives, 4, 5, 7, 11, 12, 13, 20, 22.

Every effort has been made to contact copyright holders of any material reproduced in this book. Any omissions will be rectified in subsequent printings if notice is given to the publisher.

All the Internet addresses (URLs) given in this book were valid at the time of going to press. However, due to the dynamic nature of the Internet, some addresses may have changed, or sites may have changed or ceased to exist since publication. While the author and publisher regret any inconvenience this may cause readers, no responsibility for any such changes can be accepted by either the author or the publisher.

Some words are shown in bold, **like this**. You can find out what they mean by looking in the glossary.

Contents

Aboriginal people and new settlers

Only **Aboriginal** people lived in Canada until the 1500s. They spoke many languages and lived in different areas of the country. By around 1750, thousands of Europeans had settled in eastern Canada. Most settlers were British or French.

European people arrived in Canada from the 1500s.

DID YOU KNOW?

Aboriginal people were sometimes at war with settlers from Great Britain and France. At other times, they were all good friends and some Aboriginal people helped to defend Canada.

Loyalists

In 1763 Britain won a war against France. Britain took control of many **colonies** in North America away from France. But some colonies wanted to be **independent**. They fought a war with Britain and formed the United States. Other colonists wanted to stay part of Britain. They moved north from the United States and formed **British North America**.

British North America would later become Canada.

DID YOU KNOW?

People who wanted to stay part of Britain were called **Loyalists**. They were helped by British soldiers.

War of 1812

In 1812 Great Britain and the United States went to war again. The United States wanted the British to leave North America. The British army, settlers, and **First Nations** people fought together to stop the United States sending the British away. After the war, more British settlers arrived in what would become Canada.

First Nations leaders worked with British officers to fight the United States.

The **Shawnee** helped the British defeat the Americans.

British North America in the 1800s

Most homes in **British North America** were built near water. People used this water to drink, wash with, and farm. Also, it was easier to travel on water than to travel on land. Toronto, Québec City, Kingston, and Montréal are all cities that were built beside water.

Many settlers lived in small cabins on farms. Some people lived in towns.

DID YOU KNOW?

In 1760, about 100,000 people lived in British North America. By 1850, there were over two million.

Many adults worked in farms, stores, workshops, and banks. Country children worked on farms and town children worked in stores or workshops. In 1871, a law in Ontario said that children should go to school. Parts of Canada did not pass this law until 1910. All students were expected to work in their spare time.

A common job in the town was that of a blacksmith.

DID YOU KNOW?

In their free time, people had parties with food and dancing. People also curled or played hockey or lacrosse.

Becoming a country

In 1864 eastern **British North America** had five **colonies**. Some people thought they should **unite** as:

1. Britain was busy with other colonies.
2. Many Americans wanted British North America's colonies to join them. British North America could protect itself better if it was united.
3. If the colonies worked together they could build a railroad. This would make trade easier.
4. Colonies argued instead of working together. A new country might stop the arguing.

DID YOU KNOW?

This is what North America looked like in 1864. In 1867, United Canada became Ontario and Québec. They formed a new country with New Brunswick and Nova Scotia. Prince Edward Island joined in 1873.

United States
Uncolonized land
British Colonies
Rupert's Land
United Province of Canada
New Brunswick
Nova Scotia

The leaders of the **colonies** in **British North America** met three times to talk about being one country. On July 1, 1867, Ontario, Québec, Nova Scotia, and New Brunswick became a new country called Canada. Together, they made this new country without fighting or going to war.

The men who planned the new country are called the Fathers of **Confederation**.

DID YOU KNOW?

Women and the **Aboriginal** people were not part of the planning. No one asked them to be part of the meetings.

Canada grows

It took more than one hundred years for all of the **provinces** and **territories** to become part of Canada. Nunavut became a territory in 1999.

DID YOU KNOW?

The last province to join the **Confederation** was the first **colony**, called Newfoundland and Labrador. It joined in 1949.

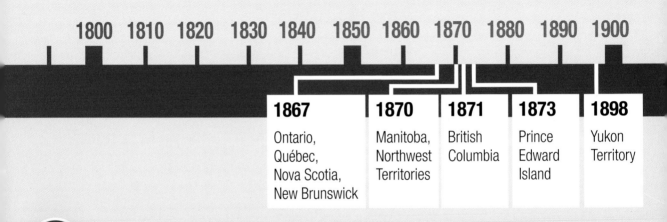

1800	1810	1820	1830	1840	1850	1860	1870	1880	1890	1900

1867
Ontario, Québec, Nova Scotia, New Brunswick

1870
Manitoba, Northwest Territories

1871
British Columbia

1873
Prince Edward Island

1898
Yukon Territory

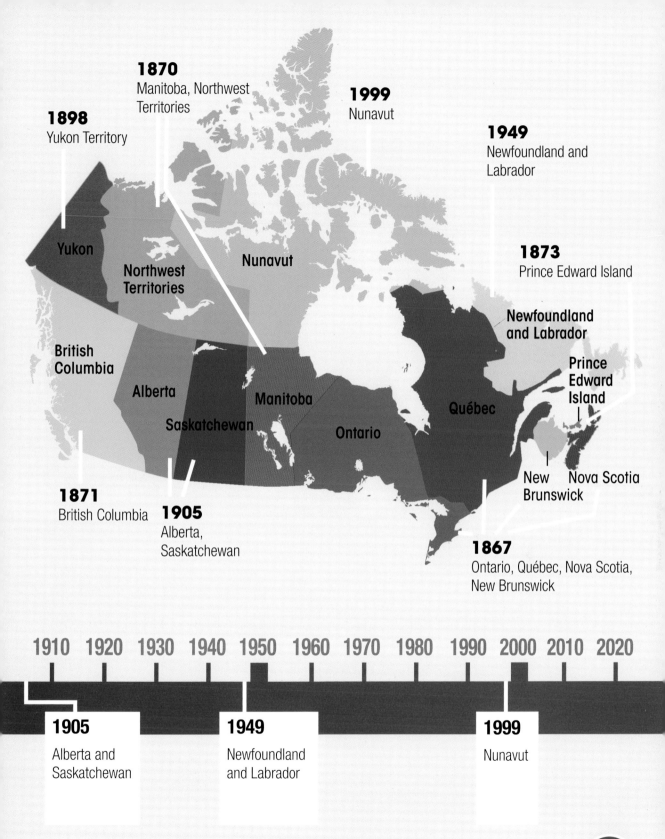

1870
Manitoba, Northwest
Territories

1999
Nunavut

1949
Newfoundland and
Labrador

1898
Yukon Territory

Yukon

Northwest
Territories

Nunavut

1873
Prince Edward Island

British
Columbia

Alberta

Newfoundland
and Labrador

Saskatchewan

Manitoba

Ontario

Québec

Prince
Edward
Island

New
Brunswick

Nova Scotia

1871
British Columbia

1905
Alberta,
Saskatchewan

1867
Ontario, Québec, Nova Scotia,
New Brunswick

1910   1920   1930   1940   1950   1960   1970   1980   1990   2000   2010   2020

1905

Alberta and
Saskatchewan

1949

Newfoundland
and Labrador

1999

Nunavut

19

Building railways

The new country of Canada was very big. It took a long time to travel between places. The Canadians needed a way to send **goods** and people between places quickly. This would help the people trade. A railway that was 1,100 km (683 miles) long was built.

In the 1800s, people often travelled by wagon or on foot. There were no cars, highways, or airplanes.

Canada's first railroad between the **provinces** opened on Canada's ninth birthday: July 1, 1876.

Railways to British Columbia

In 1871, British Columbia said they would join Canada if a railway was built. People who lived there felt very far away from Canada. Many Americans thought British Columbia should join the United States, not Canada. To stop this, the Canadian government agreed to build a railroad to connect Ontario with British Columbia.

The builders of the railway had to find ways to cross dangerous mountain passes.

Thousands of men worked to build the new railway. Many of them came from China.

British Columbia joined Canada in 1871 but waited more than ten years for a railroad. The Canadian Pacific Railway was finished in 1885. Using the new railways, Canadians could travel from sea to sea without going through the United States.

Local workers building the Canadian Pacific Railway earned up to $2.50 each day. Workers brought in from China were paid a lot less.

The railway travelled 3,200 km (1,988 miles) across Ontario, the prairies, and through the mountains.

Aboriginal people vs the railroads

Between 1870 and 1885, the **Aboriginal** people living on the prairies were unhappy. They wanted to be part of Canada but did not want to leave their lands for new settlers and railroads. First they sent letters to the government. This did not work, so they began to fight.

Louis Riel was a Métis politician who helped bring Manitoba into the **Confederation**. He is at the centre of this picture.

Each time Aboriginal people fought, the government sent troops to stop it. Finally, the **Métis** leaders surrendered. After 1885 thousands of people used the railway to travel west and settle.

Making candles

In the 1800s people used candles to light their homes. Many people made their own candles.

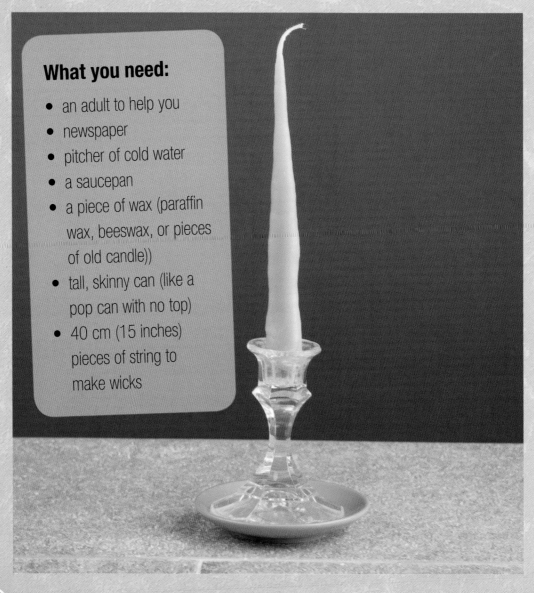

What you need:

- an adult to help you
- newspaper
- pitcher of cold water
- a saucepan
- a piece of wax (paraffin wax, beeswax, or pieces of old candle))
- tall, skinny can (like a pop can with no top)
- 40 cm (15 inches) pieces of string to make wicks

What to do:

1. Place newspaper on a surface to keep it clean.

2. Pour 6 cm (about 2 inches) of water in the saucepan.

3. Put the wax in the can. Put the can in the saucepan.

4. Have an adult help you boil this water until the wax melts.

5. When it is melted, the adult should take the pot off the stove and put it down on the newspaper.

6. Hold one end of the string and dip it into the wax. Take it out quickly.

7. Let it drip over the can. Quickly dip it in the cold water to harden. Dip it in the wax again. Each time a little more wax will stick to the candle.

8. Keep dipping until the candle is the size you want.

Glossary

Aboriginal original and ancestors of the people who live in a land; in Canada, this includes the Inuit and the Métis people

British North America colonies in North America ruled by Great Britain

colony place ruled by another country

Confederation colonies joined together to form a new country

goods things that are made and sold

independent not ruled by someone else

First Nations people who have lived in Canada for thousands of years; not Inuit or Méti

Loyalists people who wanted to remain loyal to Great Britain

Métis people whose ancestors were both European and First Nations or Inuit

province section of the country with its own government, whose power is granted by the Constitution Act

Shawnee First Nations people who occupied Eastern North America

territory section of the country with its own local government that is given power by the federal government

unite come together to form something

Find out more

Books

The Kids Book of Aboriginal Peoples in Canada, Diane Silvey and John Mantha (Kids Can Press, 2012)

The Kids Book of Canada's Railway and How the CPR Was Built, Deborah Hodge (Kids Can Press, 2008)

Websites

FactHound offers a safe, fun way to find Internet sites related to this book. All of the sites on FactHound have been researched by our staff.

Here's all you do:

Visit www.facthound.com
Type in this code: 9781410981202

Index